VERMEER
OF DELFT

Cover: Johannes Vermeer
Girl with the pearl earring
Mauritshuis, The Hague

© 2005 first edition
© 2007 second edition
© 2009 third edition
© 2012 fifth revised edition
Bekking & Blitz Publishers
PO Box 286   Koningin Astridlaan 2A
3800 AG Amersfoort   8200 Brugge
The Netherlands   Belgium

ISBN 978 90 6109 5743

VERMEER OF DELFT
1632 - 1675
His life and times

Drs. Michel van Maarseveen

Translation: M.E. Bennet

BEKKING & BLITZ UITGEVERS
Amersfoort   -   Brugge

Girl with the pearl earring, c. 1665
The Hague, Mauritshuis

Contents

View of Delft (detail) c. 1660-1661
The Hague, Mauritshuis

Preface

Ever since the Delft painter Johannes Vermeer (1632-1675) was 'rediscovered' in the nineteenth century, he has been recognised as one of the three great Dutch artists of the Golden Age. We know so much about the lives of Rembrandt van Rijn and Frans Hals, but we are in the dark as to important periods in the life of Vermeer. Nothing is known about his childhood, and we can only hazard a guess as to his apprenticeship. We have certainly learned a great deal about the life of Vermeer during the past ten years. Additional information was also provided by the American art historian Michael Montias, thanks to his painstaking and intensive research.

In this book we have chosen to approach our subject by way of location, meaning that Vermeer's life and work is described in relation to the places in Delft with which he was associated in some way.

It is sad that many of these buildings have disappeared in the three and a half centuries since Vermeer's death. The inn belonging to Vermeer's father, his house, the Guildhall where he was a member of the Board, the town gates in the *View of Delft*, were all demolished in the nineteenth century. But the last ten years of research have yielded information on new places in Delft relevant to the life of Vermeer. These include the house where he was born and the house where his father was born.

The location of Vermeer's painting *The little street* is the object of a lively ongoing discussion, with all the theories being put forward and analysed in detail.

Pieter de Hooch
Courtyard with a woman and child, *1658*
London, The National Gallery

1 Vermeer and the Delft Art of painting

Delft as a seventeenth century centre of art

In the early seventeenth century, painting in Delft was fairly mediocre. Some artists in the town portrayed biblical and mythological subjects. One of these was Leonaert Bramer (1596-1674), whose work stands out with a fluent and animated style and experiments with light. The art of portraiture, on the other hand, had reached a high level in Delft. The most important painter in this genre was Michiel Jansz. van Mierevelt (1567-1641). He was usually commissioned to portray wealthy burghers of Delft and nobles from the stadholder's court circle. The demand for portraits was so great that Van Mierevelt employed several apprentices who copied his work. There is a notable series of state portraits of the stadholders of Holland and Friesland, commissioned by the town council of Delft in 1620. Van Mierevelt's portraits are outstanding for their subtle and accurate portrayal of the face, reflecting the distinguished status of the subject with a stately charisma. His style was continued by Jacob 11 Willemsz. Delff and Willem van Vliet. Still-life painting in Delft was also popular with the artists Pieter Cornelisz. van Rijk, Balthasar van der Ast and Harmen Steenwijk. Painters in Delft were producing still-life pictures throughout the seventeenth century.

There were some big changes in painting at Delft during the 1640s. Several well-known artists settled in the town at this time. They included the painter of cattle Paulus Potter, specialists in church interiors Gerard Houckgeest and Emanuel de Witte, the folk artist Jan Steen, Rembrandt's apprentice Carel Fabritius and Pieter de Hooch, who painted interiors. Most of these artists only worked in Delft for a short time, but their presence was a great incentive to local painting, causing new genres to be taken up, including interiors, townscapes and church interiors. The Delft artist Hendrick van Vliet also painted church interiors, in addition to the two artists mentioned above. They often chose the Oude or Nieuwe Kerk interiors as their subject. Their outstanding features include strong diagonals and the use of unexpected points of view. People are often portrayed in the interiors of churches in a perfectly natural way. These new developments were at their height in the early 1650s. The artistic level dropped again soon after 1660, when many of these influential painters had left for Amsterdam, or, like Fabritius, they had died. The only great master to stay in Delft was Johannes Vermeer (1632-1675).

The development and significance of Vermeer's painting

It is no easy matter to outline the development of Vermeer's work, as only three of his paintings are dated. A reconstruction of his stylistic development can be made based on those works and by comparison with paintings by contemporaries. Vermeer's earliest works depict bible scenes and mythological subjects. While the painting *Christ in the house of Mary and Martha* was being cleaned in 1901, Vermeer's signature was uncovered. Earlier on, during restoration of Diana resting with her companions in the Mauritshuis, the letters 'J Meer' were discovered. These two finds threw new light on the work of Vermeer who, it seems, at the start of his career painted very different subjects to those in his later works. A strong Italian influence is to be seen in both paintings. There is no evidence, however, that Vermeer was ever in Italy. He may well have come to know southern painting through the Italian paintings imported during the seventeenth century and the Dutch followers of Italianate art, the Amsterdam history painters and the Caravaggisti of Utrecht. He was on good terms with Leonaert Bramer (1596-1674) who spent some time in Italy, and this contact may also have introduced him to that style of painting.

Vermeer must have been familiar with the work of Italian painters as he assessed the value of a number of paintings, believed to be Roman and Venetian, which the Brandenburg

Christ in the house of Mary and Martha, *c. 1655*
Edinbourg, National Galleries of Scotland

Diana and her compagnons, *c. 1655-1656*
The Hague, Mauritshuis

The matchmaker, *1656*
Dresden, Staatliche Kunstsammlungen
Gemäldegalerie, Alte Meister

Elector wanted to buy for a huge sum in 1671. Warned against this by his advisor Hendrik de Formanteau, the Elector decided not to buy. But the art dealer refused to take the paintings back. Fortmanteau then called in experts to demonstrate that the works were forgeries or copies. Vermeer was probably approached because he also dealt in paintings of other artists. Together with the artist Hans Jordaens he appeared before a notary at The Hague and declared the works to be a 'load of trash' worth not even a tenth of the price asked.

Between 1656 and 1658 Vermeer's work went through a period of transition. The painting *The matchmaker* forms the link between the classical and mythological subjects and the contemporary scenes he painted from then on. This painting still shows Vermeer's early monumental style, while revealing a new phase in his work by the choice of subject. Influenced by Pieter de Hooch (1629-1684) Vermeer began to concentrate on painting interiors during this period, emphasising the incidence of light and perspective. In comparison with the work of De Hooch, Vermeer simplified his paintings by concentrating on a few objects that he portrayed, paying special attention to the play of sunlight in a room. This development was first seen in the painting *A girl asleep* and was later perfected in *The girl with the wineglass*. He painted two townscapes in about 1660: *View of Delft* and *The little street*. These paintings follow developments in Delft painting in the mid-seventeenth century, with the depiction of buildings in perspective and the naturalistic painting of light as the main features. Vermeer painted robustly in this period, applying his paint lavishly, particularly in the lighter coloured areas. The figures are boldly modelled, for instance in *The milkmaid*.

His work began to show refinement and a subtler portrayal of objects from about 1662, as in *Young woman with a water jug*. Influenced by the work of Leiden artist Frans van Mieris, this tendency was continued in three small paintings of women

A girl asleep, *c. 1657*
New York, The Metropolitan Museum of Art

The little street, *c. 1657 - 1658*
Amsterdam, Rijksmuseum

View of Delft, *c. 1660-1661*
The Hague, Mauritshuis

The milkmaid, *c. 1658-1660*
Amsterdam, Rijksmuseum

standing before a table by the window: *Woman in blue reading a letter*, *A woman holding a balance* and *Woman with a pearl necklace*. Vermeer also painted people making music during this period, including *The concert*. In contrast with his earlier interior paintings the figures are placed in the background and the foreground is dominated by a heavy table.

The allegory of painting, which he painted about 1665, forms an absolute climax in Vermeer's oeuvre. In this work he flawlessly combined detailed reproduction with a sublime dimensional picture. Vermeer chose to simplify his paintings after *The allegory of painting*. The delicate transitions between areas of colour and the subtle depiction of details disappeared from his work, to be replaced by greater abstraction in the depiction of objects and a clear distinction between light and darker areas. This can be seen in *The love letter* in the Rijksmuseum and *Mistress and maid* in the Frick Collection in New York. Two outstanding paintings in Vermeer's oeuvre are *The astronomer* (1668) and *The geographer* (1669) which, together with *The matchmaker* (1656) are his only dated works. In these two works Vermeer still paints in his refined style of the early 1660s while at the same time introducing austerity, for instance in the background.

The best works in this new style were painted about 1670 and include *The lace maker*, in which the artist concentrates on portraying human diligence to the exclusion of everything else. During the last years of his life Vermeer's paintings again portray music, as in *A lady standing at the virginal* and *A lady seated at the virginal*. This time he painted only women with their instruments, whereby the woman herself is the central figure, no longer just a person in a room, as she was ten years earlier.

Vermeer worked very slowly. He could not accomplish more than two or three paintings a year because of his extremely painstaking way of painting. Thirty-one works have been preserved which can be firmly attributed to Vermeer and there are four or five about which there is some doubt. Taking into

Young woman with a water jug, *c. 1664-1665*
New York, Metropolitan Museum of Art

A woman holding a balance, *c. 1664*
Washington, National Gallery of Art, Widener collection

Woman with a pearl necklace, *c. 1664*
Berlin, Gemäldegalerie staatliche Museen zu Berlin

23

account that some paintings have been lost, Vermeer's complete works are thought to number between forty and fifty. This is a very small number when compared with the productivity of Rembrandt or Frans Hals. The following incident shows how slowly he worked: the French diplomat Balthazar de Monconys came to Delft in 1663, when he also visited Vermeer. Not one of his paintings was to be seen in his studio. To see one of the works he had to go to a Delft baker's shop (probably Hendrick van Buyten, who possessed four paintings by Vermeer). Vermeer worked mainly for local clients. The wealthy Pieter van Ruijven of Delft (1624-1674) had the largest collection; he bought about half of Vermeer's oeuvre (i.e. fifteen works) between 1657 and 1675. As long as his paintings stayed in the houses of Delft, he remained quite unknown. Even so, his work was held in high esteem. When his paintings began to circulate outside Delft at the end of the seventeenth century, they fetched high prices.

The significance of Vermeer's work is to be found in the systematic development of themes and techniques introduced by other artists. Vermeer was certainly no great innovator, but he could raise the findings of others to a far higher plane. This gave his work its strength.

Woman in blue, reading a letter, *c. 1663-1664*
Amsterdam, Rijksmuseum

The love letter, *c. 1669-1670*
Amsterdam, Rijksmuseum

Mistress and maid, *c. 1667*
New York, Frick Collection

A lady standing at the virginal, *c. 1672-1673*
London, National Gallery

A lady seated at the virginal, *c. 1675*
London, National Gallery

The music lesson, *ca. 1662-1664*
London, Buckingham Palace.

A girl playing the guitar, *c. 1670*
Kenwood, The Iveagh Bequest Trust

A girl playing the lute, *c. 1664*
New York, The Metropolitan Museum of Art

The astronomer, *1668*
Paris, Musée du Louvre

The géographer, *1669*
Frankfurt am Main, Städelsches
Kunstinstitut

The allegory of painting. *c.1666-1667*
Vienna, Kunsthistorische Museum

The lace maker, *c. 1669-1670*
Paris, Musée du Louvre

The Voldersgracht and surroundings, detail from the Figurative Map*, 1675-1678*
On the Voldersgracht are
a) the Flying Fox, where Vermeer
lived the first years of his life;
b) The Mechelen Inn, where
he grew up and
c) the Guild of St. Luke, of which
he was a member

2 The young artist

The Flying Fox Inn

Vermeer's parents, Reynier Jansz. and Digna Baltens, probably moved house in the late 1620s. They may have lived somewhere else after The Three Hammers Inn was let in 1624, but it is certain that the couple lived on the Voldersgracht in 1631. They rented an inn there, complete with a sign depicting a flying fox. Reynier combined his duties as innkeeper with his old profession of 'caffa weaver', as shown in various notarial documents in which he is described as innkeeper and caffa worker. On 13th October 1631 Reynier Jansz. enrolled with the guild of St. Luke as an art dealer, which gave him the right to buy and sell paintings. Records show that Reynier was in contact with many artists in Delft, such as Balthasar van der Ast and Jan Baptista van Fornenburgh who painted floral arrangements, the still-life artist Pieter Steenwijck and the landscape artist Pieter Groenewegen. Having neglected to pay a peat seller for a load of peat, Reynier Jansz. became involved with the man's son-in-law after his death; this was the noted portrait and interior artist Antonie Palamedes. In 1632, a year after enrolling with the guild of St. Luke, Reynier's son Johannes Vermeer was born. (A daughter was born in 1620). Vermeer was most probably born in The Flying Fox Inn, but the exact date is unknown. Reynier was then forty-one years old and Digna was thirty-seven. The couple had already been married for seventeen years.

We know nothing about Vermeer's youth. There is no trace of the artist until his engagement in 1653. But we may assume that Johannes played outside on the Voldersgracht and the nearby Markt as a small boy. In the Flying Fox Inn there were five fireplaces on the premises, which indicates that it was quite big. It was situated on the north side of the Voldersgracht, now number 25. The inn was the third house on the east side of the Oudemannenhuis (old men's home), not

25, Voldersgracht.
This house was an Inn, called the Flying Fox during the 17th century.
Johannes Vermeer was born here in October 1632

the second, as Montias states in his book on Vermeer. We can verify this from the taxation register of 1632 and the book of fireplaces of 1638.

Reynier Jansz. signed a tenancy agreement for the inn with its owner, Pieter Corstiaensz Hopprus, a prosperous shoemaker and tanner.

The Nieuwe Kerk (the new church)

Johannes Vermeer was baptised in the Nieuwe Kerk on 31st October 1632. Witnesses to the ceremony were Pieter Brammer, Jan Heijndrickxc. and Maertge Jansdr. Pieter Brammer is unknown, Jan Heijndrickxz. was probably a picture-framer and business associate of Vermeer's father and Maertge Jansdr. was Vermeer's aunt. Only the artist's Christian name, 'Joannes' was entered in the baptismal regis-

Coenraad Decker, **De Nieuwe Kerk**, *c. 1680. Delft record office. Vermeer was baptized in the Nieuwe Kerk on 31st October 1632*

ter of the Nieuwe Kerk. The origin of the name 'Vermeer' is
not known. The first time it appears in records is on 6th April
1625 when Vermeer's paternal uncle took his daughter Neeltje
to be baptised in the Nieuwe Kerk, giving his own name as
Antonij Jansz. Vermeer. Vermeer's father did not use the name
until later in life. He first took the name of Van der Minne, the
family name of his stepfather, Claes Costiaensz. Later, when he
rented The Flying Fox Inn on the Voldersgracht, he called himself Reynier Vos, perhaps as a pun on the fable of Reynard the
Fox. From about 1640 onwards he was known as Reynier
Vermeer.

Vermeer's elder sister Geertruy was also baptissed in the
Nieuwe Kerk, on 15th March 1620. Maertge Jansdr. was wit-
ness then just as she was now for Geertruy's brother. The
Nieuwe Kerk was the scene of baptisms in the Vermeer family, but they also buried their dead there. Vermeer's paternal
grandfather Jan Reyersz. was buried there on 2nd May 1597,
his father Reinier Jansz. on 12th October 1652 and his mother
Digna Baltens on 13th February 1670.

Mechelen House

Vermeer's parents moved house when he was nine years old.
In April 1641 Reynier Jansz. bought a large house, the
Mechelen Inn on the Markt, at the corner with the Oude
Manhuissteeg. The inn had large windows facing onto the
Markt and no fewer than six fireplaces, which made Mechelen
House one of the most imposing buildings on the Markt.
Reynier had to take out two mortgages to finance the purcha-
se.

The Mechelen Inn was the bustling heart of the town. Its location, with the town hall on one side and the Nieuwe Kerk on
the other side, was very favourable and an ideal meeting place
for discussions and exchanging news. The archives show that
many Delft artists also used to meet here. Reynier Jansz. knew
Evert van Aelst, the uncle and master of the painter Willem

van Aelst; Emanuel de Witte had also been apprenticed to him. Egbert van der Poel, who painted the devastation caused by the powder explosion in Delft many times; and Leonaert Bramer, who may have been Vermeer's master, were both in touch with Reynier. His membership of the guild of St. Luke and his activities as an art dealer would certainly have had a great influence on Vermeer's artistic development, which began in earnest in Mechelen House.

It has already been mentioned in the preface that we have no information concerning Vermeer's youth or his apprenticeship. For over a hundred years the Delft archives have been searched for clues to his training, to this day without success.

The town hall of Delft, during the renovation c. 1960 the façade was restored in its original seventeenth-century state

Many of the artists known to Vermeer could have been his master, for instance the portrait and genre painter Gerard Ter Borch, Evert van Aelst and Carel Fabritius, who was ten years older than Vermeer. Others could be considered, including Willem van Vliet, the famous Delft portrait painter Jacob 11 Willemsz. Delff, Leonaert Bramer, Hans Jordaens, Balthasar van der Ast, Willem van Aelst, Antonie Palamedes, Pieter de Hooch and Frans van Mieris. It may well be that Vermeer left Delft to study elsewhere, in Amsterdam or Utrecht, for example. The artist Abraham Bloemaert, who was related to Vermeer's wife, worked in Utrecht. Vermeer may have been apprenticed to him when he met his future wife Catharina Bolnes. But we cannot be sure of anything concerning Vermeer's training until the archives yield fresh information. When Vermeer's father died in 1652, Digna Baltens carried on running her husband's inn. The inheritance cannot have amounted to much.

It is not known where Vermeer settled after his marriage in 1653, but it is generally assumed that the couple moved in with his mother at the inn on the Markt, although there is no evidence to support this. We know Vermeer's address for certain from 1660, when he was living with his mother-in-law Maria Thins, in her house on the Oude Langendijk.

Digna tried to sell Mechelen House at auction in 1669. She had set a reserve price of three thousand seven hundred guilders which was not reached, so the house was withdrawn from auction. As a result of this failure she let the inn to Leendert van Ackerdyk, who paid a hundred and ninety guilders per annum for it. Digna Baltens moved in with her daughter Geertruy, who lived in the Vlamingstraat. She died there on the 10th or 11Th of February 1670. The inn passed to Vermeer after her death. He let Mechelen House again at the beginning of 1673, to his namesake the schoolteacher Johannes van der Meer, who paid a hundred and sixty guilders per annum. Mechelen House was pulled down in 1885 to widen the Oude

Mannensteeg, which connects the Markt to the Voldersgracht. In 1955 a memorial tablet was placed in the wall of the adjoining house at number 52 the Markt, to mark the spot where Mechelen House once stood. The Delft sculptor Joh. Bijsterveld made the memorial tablet, which bears the following inscription: 'Here stood Mechelen House where the artist Jan Vermeer was born in 1632''. This contains two mistakes. Vermeer was certainly not born in Mechelen House, as his parents moved there when he was already nine years old. The name Jan is not entirely correct either. Vermeer never used the name himself. He always signed deeds with Joannes, Joannis or Johannis. Criticism was heard on all sides in 1955, but the foundation 'Delft binnen de veste' (Delft within the ramparts) which devised the inscription, decided that the Christian name Jan had become more familiar.

The town hall

The first record concerning Johannes Vermeer, after his entry in the baptismal registry of the Nieuwe Kerk, is a testimony dated 5th April 1653, drawn up by request of the artist and his future wife, Catharina Bolnes. The document states that Catharina's mother, Maria Thins, did not approve of her daughter's suitor, but that she would not stand in the way of their marriage. One of the witnesses to this statement was Leonaert Bramer. The young couple went to the town hall to proclaim the banns on the same day that Bramer made the statement. Entries of this kind were made in three registers in the seventeenth century: The civil register at the town hall, and the registers of banns of the Nieuwe Kerk and the Oude Kerk. Neither of the church registers for the period from 1650-1656 has been preserved, so we are dependent on the civil register. A note in the margin reads: 'Certificate issued at Schipluij (Schipluiden) on 20th April 1653'. This indicates that the marriage took place at Schipluiden, a village south of Delft where many Catholics lived. The Jesuits held Roman Catholic services there openly. Vermeer's in-laws were Catholic and Maria Thins had close connections with the Jesuits. This may have been the reason why the young couple was married at Schipluiden. Vermeer, who was brought up a Protestant, must have converted to Catholicism to receive the Catholic sacraments of holy matrimony. This he must have done between 5th April, when Bramer testified on behalf of Vermeer, and 20th April 1653, their wedding day. It is possible that Maria's doubts about her daughter's marriage sprang from the fact that Vermeer was a Protestant. It could also be that this wealthy lady thought that an impecunious and unknown artist was a thoroughly undesirable match for her daughter.

Coenraad Decker, the town hall, *c. 1680.*
Delft record office

3 Vermeer of Delft

Vermeer's house

Vermeer lived for a large part of his life with his family in the house of his mother-in-law, Maria Thins, at the Molenpoort corner of the Oude Langendijk , now the Jozefstraat. It is not known when Vermeer moved in there. The register of burials of the Oude Kerk shows that the artist was living at the Oude Langendijk in December 1660. It is not likely that he would have done so when he was first married. The fact that Vermeer was not able to pay his enrolment fee for the guild of St. Luke in December 1953 points to this. He did not pay it until three years later. If he had been living with his well-to-do mother-in-law she would surely have advanced him the six guilders, if only to help her daughter. Also, the fact that his mother-in-law was not at all happy with her daughter's husband at first, makes it unlikely that Vermeer and his wife lived on the Oude Langendijk during the first years of their marriage.

Vermeer's mother-in-law was always a great help to the family, often supporting them financially. Vermeer and his wife had fifteen children altogether (four of them died in infancy) and this large family was a heavy financial burden.

Thanks to an inventory made two months after his death, we have ample information on the rooms and the layout of Vermeer's house. There was a vestibule on the ground floor with a painting by Fabritius on the wall. Behind this was the big hall containing two more portraits by Fabritius. There was a small cabinet next to the big hall. Also on the ground floor were two kitchens, a scullery, a washhouse, a corridor, a cellar room, a courtyard and a small room between the ground floor and the first floor. There were a front room and a back room on the upper floor. The front room was appointed to be the studio facing north. Painters were advised in manuals to choose a studio facing north, to keep the sunlight out of their work area. It was long considered impossible to reproduce naked sunlight shining into a room. The Delft painters demonstrated that the opposite is true. In Vermeer's studio the notary's clerk listed the inventory as two easels, three palettes, six brushes, three bare canvases, one desk and three bundles of assorted prints, which were probably used as models.

Most of the rooms described in the inventory were on the ground floor, so it is most likely that Vermeer lived in this part of the house with his family, and that he worked upstairs, with Maria Thins occupying the rest of the upper floor.

It is often noted that the serenity radiating from Vermeer's paintings contrasts sharply with his busy domestic life and the incidents between his in-laws, Vermeer's brother-in-law Willem Bolnes on the one hand, and his wife and mother-in-law on the other hand. William had chosen the side of his father after his parents' divorce, and he stayed in Gouda. He visited Delft in 1663 to acknowledge a debt to his mother which seems to have started a quarrel, because eyewitnesses reported that William had more than once caused a dreadful commotion in front of Maria Thin's house, and that he had continually threatened to beat his pregnant sister Catharina with a stick. About a year after William Bolnes' outburst, Maria Thins obtained permission from the town council to have her son confined in a private 'house of correction' in the Vlamingstraat. It is probable that he stayed there until his death, a few months after Vermeer died.

The church of the Jesuits

There was a Jesuit church next to the house where Vermeer lived with his family in the seventeenth century. In those days Catholics belonged to a tolerated minority, living mainly in Paepenhoeck (Pope's corner), around the Oude Langendijk. A drawing made by Abraham Rademaker at the beginning of the eighteenth century shows the 'conventicle' of the Jesuits. The house with two figures entering it is the church as it was in the time of Vermeer. The extension on the right was added in 1678.

Allegory of painting, c. 1671-1674.
New York, The Metropolitan Museum of Art. The obvious glorification of the catholic faith in this painting suggests that is was made for a catholic patron, possible the Jesuits

Part of Vermeer's house may be visible on the far right, while the building on the left was the house of the Jesuits and the school that Vermeer's children may have attended.

That Vermeer and his family were fervent Catholics is evident from the fact that one of his children was named Ignatius after Ignatius Loyola, the founder of the Jesuit Order. A remarkable picture painted by Vermeer towards the end of his life also

Abraham Rademaker, The church of the Jesuits, *c. 1700*
Delft record office

denotes his religious convictions. The work, *Allegory of the faith* finishes with Calvinism by way of symbolism, while simultaneously glorifying Catholicism. A woman sits at the centre, her eyes raised pathetically to heaven, her right foot on a globe. There is a snake in the foreground (perhaps a symbol of Protestant heresy) with blood pouring from its mouth, in the throes of being crushed by a stone - a reference to the rock on which Peter built the church of Rome. The explicit commentary on the religious situation in the Netherlands suggests that the work was probably commissioned. The Jesuits have often been mentioned in connection with this painting.

St. Luke's Guildhall

Just six months after his marriage, on 29th December 1653, when he was twenty-one years old, Vermeer presented himself for membership of the guild of St. Luke as a master artist. Delft artists, like craftsmen and trades people, belonged to their own guild. Their patron was the evangelist Luke who, according to tradition, once painted Mary with the Christ-child. The enrolment fee was six guilders, of which Vermeer paid one and a half guilders. His financial position was evidently so poor that he was not able to pay the whole fee at once. He did not pay the remainder until two and a half years later, on 24th July

1656. The guild of St. Luke must have been founded in the Middle Ages, but it was first mentioned in documents in 1545. It was the most important and biggest guild in Delft. It was composed of artists, house painters and decorators, glass engravers, stained-glass workers, glaziers, potters, embroiderers, carpet weavers, sculptors, engravers, booksellers, printers and art dealers. The guild promoted the interests of its members, while also supervising the quality of their work. Only those artists who belonged to the guild had the right to sell their works in Delft. Delft painters, in contrast with glaziers and potters, were not obliged to submit a masterpiece, but they had to complete their six years of apprenticeship before enrolling with the guild. The Board of the guild of St. Luke comprised of six members (two potters, two stained-glass artists and two painters) under the leadership of a dean who was a member of the council of forty, a municipal advisory body. The members of the Board were appointed for a two-year period. Every year on St. Luke's day (18th October) the members of the guild chose three new Board members (one from each discipline). Two candidates were nominated for every vacancy, from which the Mayor and Aldermen made their choice before the end of the year. Vermeer was a Member of the Board twice during his life. He was chosen in 1662 at the age of thirty, one of the youngest Board members in the history of the guild. He held the position again from 1671 to 1673. The guild flourished and this is apparent by the occupation of a new guildhall on the Voldersgracht.

The guild was granted the use of the chapel of the former Old men's home in 1661, which had been in use as the cloth makers' and serge hall. The cloth makers' guild was then transferred to the Prinsenhof. The former chapel was extensively renovated. On the canal side, the building was given a classicist façade with a pediment and mullioned windows. In it was a bust of Apelles, the legendary painter from Antiquity. Below it were the coats of arms of the town of Delft, the guild

G. Lamberts, View of St. Luke's guildhall
from the Oude Manhuissteeg, *1820*
Delft record office

of St. Luke and the dean of the guild in 1661, Dirk Meerman. Striking features of the guildhall were four sculptured white-stone garlands, displaying the tools and products of the four main crafts represented by the guild: the glaziers, booksellers, potters and of course, the artists. The members decorated the interior themselves. The two Board members representing the painters in 1661, Leonaert Bramer and Cornelis de Man, painted a fresco on the ceiling and a large mantel painting respectively for the guildhall. Adriaen van de Velde and Arent van Saenen, members representing the glaziers, made all the windows, while the potters donated ten chairs upholstered with Russian leather.

The guild of St. Luke was dissolved in 1833. The guildhall fell into disrepair and when it was pulled down in 1876, and a school built on the site. The four garlands were transferred to the Rijksmuseum in Amsterdam, where they were built into the walls of the 'Fragmentengebouw'. The handsome pediment with the bust of Apelles and three coats of arms had already disappeared by that time. The Jan Vermeer school now stands in the place of the guildhall.

The 'Doelen' or shooting range of the Delft civic guard
Very little is known about Vermeer's activities apart from his painting. His name was discovered recently on a list of civic guards dated 1664. The most important duty of the civic guard was to defend the town. Guards were expected to assist in keeping public order in emergency situations. All able-bodied men of some substance were obliged to take part in the exercises of the guard. The Delft civil guard was reorganised in 1580 by order of William of Orange. The town was divided into four quarters, each with its own company, referred to by the colour of its banner. The Green, Orange, White and Blue companies were formed with a captain at the head of each, assisted by a lieutenant, an ensign and two or three sergeants. A company consisted of six squads of thirty-two guards. Vermeer was a guard in the Orange company. An inventory from 1676 shows

that he was equipped with armour, a helmet and a pike. Under the leadership of Captain Van Hurk, he went to Gouda on 8th May 1673 to fight the French troops who had invaded the Netherlands. After 1655 the Delft civil guard met in the new 'Doelen' or shooting range on the Verwersdijk. The old Doelen building had been destroyed in the powder explosion of 1654, along with some of their group portraits. Only four of these could be restored. The town council put the site of the former convent of Mary Magdalene at the disposal of the Delft civil guard for their new accommodation. Leonaert Bremer was commissioned to paint mural decorations in the hall. Bramer was a sergeant in the same company as Vermeer. There is a triptych by Bramer in Stedelijk Museum the Prinsenhof, which was probably the draft design for these murals. The Doelen was demolished in 1830 to be replaced by a theatre, which has also disappeared in the meantime.

The little street, *c. 1657-1658 (detail)*
Amsterdam, Rijksmuseum

4 Where was Vermeer's Little Street?

The painting

One of Vermeer's most famous works is *The little street*, which was donated to the Rijksmuseum in 1921 by the oil magnate Henry W. A. Deterding, to celebrate his twenty-fifth anniversary as director of the Royal Dutch Petroleum Company. The painting was dated on the basis of stylistic analysis about 1658. An auction catalogue of 1696 reveals that Vermeer painted another, similar, picture. It mentions a *View of a house in Delft* and *a View of several houses*. *The little street* is usually identified with the first of these works. The little street portrays parts of two façades in Delft, seen from a slightly raised viewpoint. A woman sits in the doorway of the house on the right, bent over her embroidery or lace-making. Two children are absorbed in play on the chequered pavement in front of the house. Vermeer had originally painted a fifth figure by the open archway. We can only see a small part of the house on the left. The top of the roof slopes steeply, becoming less steep by the dormer window. A roof of this kind with a kink in it indicates that the house has a side room. There are two triangular gables in the background of the painting. The house behind the left-hand gable, to which the closed archway seems to lead, must be very big. The gable on the right, further back, is probably the back of a house facing onto a canal running parallel. The painting evokes a serene atmosphere, with people quietly engaged in everyday activities. Sewing and cleaning the house were considered examples of work for virtuous women in the seventeenth century, and so was childcare. The grapevine against the house on the left, which has been associated with loyalty, love and marriage since antiquity, may be an allusion to this. The figures in the painting are secondary to their environment. This can be seen in the perfectly accurate depiction of the bricks and the vegetation, while the face of the woman in the doorway is unrecognisable. The mainly blue colouring of the vine is caused by oxidation of the yellow pigment in paint which was originally green. This is also the case with the trees in *View of Delft*. The two archways connecting the houses to each other catch the eye in this painting. Whatever is behind the door of the archway on the left remains hidden from view. It probably belonged to the house on the left, or it may have led to the buildings behind the two houses. The archway on the right is open, allowing us to see into the courtyard. Peep-through views into depth like this are often to be seen in the work of Pieter de Hooch. The way in which Vermeer accentuated the bricks by drawing white lines of varying thickness along a reddish brown foundation is a technique he borrowed from De Hooch, who also used it. A maid is at work in the courtyard by a rain tub. A little gulley in front of the tub is glistening with water. The fact that the gulley runs through the paving indicates that the houses are situated along a canal. The incidence of light in the painting suggests that the canal ran from east to west and that the house stood on the north side of the water. The house on the right, of which we can see most of the façade, has some architectural features indicating that it was built before the town fire of 1536. For instance the construction of the façade, the high recessed alcove and the crenulated steps of the stepped gable. The many cracks, patched up here and there, also reveal the ripe old age of the house. The accurate reproduction of the brickwork and the cracks in places where they are to be expected constructionally, indicate that Vermeer chose an existing location to start with.

Then again, Vermeer seems to have made several adjustments to the façade. The doorway of the house on the right is not in the centre but slightly to the left, so that the entrance is nearer to the left window than to the right window. An explanation for this could be that there was a side room in the right-hand part of the front, separated from the rest of the house. The underside of the window frame on the right of the first floor is a little higher than the one on the left, making the shutter on the right-hand window shorter than the other two shutters. The same applies to the two windows on the ground floor. Moreover, the shutter on the window to the right of the door is narrower than the two shutters of the left-hand window. This would mean that the window frame on the right is smaller than the one on the left. The thin sidewall of the house on the right is also remarkable. The windows are topped by half-moon arches which conduct the weight of the façade downwards on a slope. This causes lateral pressure on the wall next to the window frame. The outer wall of the house on the right is of single-brick thickness, too narrow to adequately withstand the horizontal load. The house would need a timber frame to support this. Since Deterding made his donation, historians and art historians have turned their attention to the question where in Delft the houses in the painting must be located. Some presumed that Vermeer had a particular reason for painting the houses on *The little street*, but there is no evidence to support this. So many Delft scenes were painted during the seventeenth century, but hardly ever with a reason for choosing a particular location. It may have been commissioned by the owner, Pieter van Ruijven, so that the houses in the painting are not connected so much with Vermeer, as with his patron. An astonishing amount of research has been carried out during this century into the possible location in Delft of *The little street*.

Although most of the resulting theories had to be rejected at a later stage, they are interesting enough to be recorded here. Seven theories were put forward, of which three still stand: 24-25-26 Nieuwe Langendijk, 19-20 Voldersgracht, and the recent idea concerning 21 Voldersgracht. The other four have been rejected due to incorrect interpretation of the facts.

25 Oude Langendijk

The Delft municipal archivist Mr. L.G.N. Bouricius was one of the first to devote himself to the location of *The little street*. In 1922 he put forward the theory that Vermeer had painted his house on the Oude Langendijk and that the two archways stood where the Molenpoort was (now Jozefstraat). Vermeer would then have painted *The little street* from the rear of one of the houses on the Markt. The perspective in the painting reveals that the artist's viewpoint was one and a half meters above ground level.

The houses on the Markt have a low-lying kitchen by the water at the rear, with a room over it above ground level, but below the first floor: in short, this must have been the artist's viewpoint. But Bouricius' theory does not fit the facts. Until the nineteen sixties it was always thought that this house stood at the west corner of the Oude Langendijk and the Molenpoort (now Jozefstraat), where number 25 now stands. Research in the archives has revealed in two different ways that Vermeer's house stood on the other side, the east side of the Molenpoort and not on the south side like the houses in the picture. It also appears from the inventory of 1676 that his house must have been much bigger than the premises at number 25. Apart from being the wrong locality for Vermeer's house, old maps of Delft show that there were never two archways side by side on this spot. That would have been most unlikely because the Molenpoort was a road linking the Burgwal to the Nieuwe Langendijk, while the two archways in the painting clearly have no such purpose.

1 Spieringstraat

In his book about painting in Delft of 1948, the Delft journalist J.H. Oosterloo suggested the southern corner of the Spieringstraat with the Vijverstraat as a possible location for Vermeer's painting, as he saw some likeness to it. The situation certainly resembles The Little street, but the Spieringstraat was not a canal, the houses are on the west side instead of the north side and the house is not old enough either, so that Oosterloo's theory becomes most unlikely.

21 Voldersgracht

In his book on Vermeer of 1950, the Dutch art historian P.T.A. Swillens suggested that Vermeer may have painted *The little street* from the back of the Mechelen Inn, his parents' home on the Markt which faced onto the Voldersgracht. The houses surrounding the Markt have an upper room at the rear so that the raised perspective would fit in any case. According to Swillens, the Home for old men and women stood on that site on the Voldersgracht and was pulled down in 1661, to be replaced by the new accommodation for the guild of St. Luke. This was in the same period that Vermeer painted *The little street* and Swillens thought that Vermeer wanted to record the scene before it was demolished. The building on the right of the painting would be the old people's home and the two women were inmates. In that case the archway on the right in the painting disappeared during the renovations, while the left-hand archway can still be seen on the drawing made by Abraham Rademaker in about 1700. Swillens' interpretation was severely criticised as soon as his book was published. Firstly, only the old men's home stood on the Voldersgracht; the old women's home was in the Papenstraat, now the 'Huyse van St. Christoffel'. Secondly, the old men's home was not demolished as Swillens thought, but renovated. It has often been assumed in literature concerning Vermeer that he had his studio in his parents' house. This could be true, but there is no evidence for it. Vermeer's studio could just as well have been in the house of his mother-in-law on the Oude Langendijk, where the artist and his family were living in 1660, and perhaps even earlier. A fourth argument against Swillens' theory is the fact that the

47, Achterom
This building is associated with The little street,
but a closer look reveals that its front is much smaller

22, Vlamingstraat

house on the right of Vermeer's painting almost certainly dates from before the town fire of 1536. This fire, which reduced a large part of Delft to ashes, probably destroyed the houses on the Voldersgracht. A town plan of Delft painted after the fire shows the extent of the damage. According to this painting, there is nothing left of the houses on the Voldersgracht, but we must add that the damage shown in the plan may have been exaggerated. Archaeological research revealed that the damage was not as great as the painting suggests. However, as the Voldersgracht was at the centre of destruction, the houses on this side of the canal may well have disappeared. It is obvious that the houses painted by Vermeer were in another part of the town.

22 *Vlamingstraat*

After attending a lecture on Vermeer in 1957, the owner of the premises at 22 Vlamingstraat at the time, felt sure that he was living in the house painted by Vermeer in *The little street*. The longer he looked at the painting, the more convinced he became, and when he also learned that Vermeer's mother lived in the Vlamingstraat during her last years, this decided the matter for him. The woman in the archway could be no other than Digna Baltens. He had forgotten that Vermeer's mother lived in Mechelen House on the Markt until 1659, while the painting was dated about 1658. The house in the Vlamingstraat certainly bears a strong resemblance to the house in *The little street*. In the eighteenth century it housed an inn called the 'Hof van Holland'. There is a picture of the inn on a late eighteenth-century brass tobacco tin in The Prinsenhof Stedelijk Museum. The layout of the frontage, the shape of the windows and the archway on the left correspond with the painting. The house even stands on the north side of the canal, but the theory is undermined by the absence of a double archway. It is precisely this detail, in combination with the other conditions, which narrows down the number of possible locations in Delft.

22-24-26 *Nieuwe Langendijk*

Archaeological and architectural research took place in three houses on the Nieuwe Langendijk during 1982. The information unearthed during this research also concerns *The little street*. Based on this, the municipal archaeological historian W.F. Weve put forward the theory that Vermeer had chosen this location for his painting. This part of the Nieuwe Langendijk meets the basic requirements: the houses are situated on the north side of an east-west running canal, on the edge of that part of town which was spared by the fire of 1536. It is quite possible that there were still some late mediaeval houses there in the seventeenth century.

The three houses on the Nieuwe Langendijk were pulled

down in 1982. Number 26, dating from the second half of the fifteenth century, was the most easterly of the houses. It was of the same construction and proportions as the house on the right of the painting. Number 22 corresponds with the part under the steeply pitched roof of the house on the left, while the house at number 24, dating from the first half of the nineteenth century, stood on the site of the two archways and the side room of the house on the left of the painting. There was a large hall behind numbers 22 and 24 dating from the first half of the fifteenth century, with dimensions and layout corresponding with the house on the left in the background of the

22-24-26, Nieuwe Langendijk,
before the demolition in 1982.
Delft record office

painting. It was a great disappointment during the excavations that the soil underneath number 24 had been seriously disturbed. The sewer and a shallow cellar had churned up the soil to a depth of half a meter below ground level. In addition the excavation of the building had to be carried out in so short a time that it was impossible to determine whether there had been two archways on this spot in the seventeenth century. Sadly, soil research at number 24 failed to produce proof of this theory. All the same, the archaeological research and finds fitted in with Weve's theory, making it more plausible. This is remarkable enough in itself because there are so few places in Delft which meet all the demands made by the painting regarding its location. Moreover, this is the only theory which takes the houses in the background of the painting into account. This is neglected in all the other hypotheses on *The little street*. Our hope is now concentrated on research into the residential history of the houses on 22-26 Nieuwe Langendijk, which could reveal that Vermeer had some kind of connection with this location. Dubious as this may be, it is the only possibility of supporting the argument for the Nieuwe Langendijk. The problem is that research into the residential history of an old building is an extremely accurate and painstaking activity with no guarantee that it will eventually yield the names of former inhabitants. As yet, no-one has taken it upon themselves to carry out research of this kind on the Nieuwe Langendijk.

19 and 20 Voldersgracht

A fresh attempt to locate *The little street* on the Voldersgracht was made by Mrs. M.A. Lindenburg in 1993. Mrs. Lindenburg followed up Swillens theory, which held that Vermeer painted the houses on the Voldersgracht from Mechelen house, about one and a half metres above street level, but she located the houses slightly more to the west at numbers 19 and 20. This means that the house on the left of Abraham Rademaker's drawing of the guildhall is the house on the right in the painting by Vermeer. Both houses share the same arrangement of the façade, with the characteristic high window over the front door. The two archways in the painting would still be in existence. The archway on the right actually leads in to a courtyard, while the one on the left is now built into the façade of number 19, but it does not belong there and until recently it still had a paved surface. Another interesting detail is that the artist Cornelis Daemen Rietwijck lived at number 20 and gave lessons in drawing, mathematics and other subjects there.

Perhaps Vermeer learned the rudiments of drawing from him. However attractive Mrs. Lindenburg's theory may be, there are a few snags to it. Vermeer could see the two houses from the rear window of the Mechelen Inn, but he would not have been able to see into the archway. This is only possible from the back of the premises at 50 the Markt, two houses further along. In that case Vermeer must have adjusted the perspective. At this point an inconsistency crops up in the theory, which assumes that Vermeer's viewpoint must have been above street level. Assuming that Vermeer adjusted the perspective horizontally, he could have done the same vertically. Moreover, if Vermeer wanted to paint the view from his studio, he would have been more likely to choose the houses straight in front of it, in this case the old men's home, than the houses which he could only see from the northeast corner of his studio. A third argument against Mrs. Lindenburg's theory is that the fire of 1536 most probably destroyed the houses on the Voldersgracht, while the house on the right of *The little street* is almost sure to have been built before the fire. Mrs. Lindenburg's theory turns out to be less plausible than it seems at first sight.

21 Voldersgracht reviewed

In the catalogue of the 1995/1996 Vermeer exhibition in the National Gallery in Washington and the Mauritshuis in The

Hague, the authors Arthur Wheelock and Ben Broos suggest that Vermeer may have composed the houses in *The little street* using elements from several different buildings. Just as Pieter de Hooch combined various pieces of architecture into a seemingly realistic environment in his paintings of Delft courtyards, Vermeer could also have composed the houses in his painting from separate elements. De Hooch's method was easy to trace because he painted several comparable works in which the same constructional elements were used continually, in a different context. *The little street* is unique within what was preserved of Vermeer's oeuvre, so that no one considered this possibility. Both authors stress the asymmetrical construction of the façade with shutters and window frames of varying sizes to support their theory. The fact that the houses in the picture are only partly visible suggests that Vermeer did not set out to paint an accurate 'portrait' of an existing house.

Wheelock and Broos try to discover what Vermeer's main source of inspiration could have been. They fall back on Swillens' idea that Vermeer painted what he saw from the back of the Mechelen Inn, again putting forward 21 Voldersgracht. There are drawings and prints of St. Luke's guildhall, which show a narrow entrance with an awning on the left. Next to this are a mullioned window and an archway. According to both authors, Vermeer took this part of the guildhall as the basis for *The little street*, and the rest of the frontage in the painting must have stood in another part of the Voldersgracht.

However plausible this theory seems, it is not very probable. The precise brushwork and the sound construction of the façade with all kinds of details, such as the chimney just visible between the two merlons on the right, make it far more likely that Vermeer painted an existing house and that he modified some parts of it to improve the composition. He worked along similar lines in *View of Delft*.

5 The View of Delft

The location of View of Delft

Vermeer's most famous painting is without a doubt the monumental *View of Delft*, which he probably painted in, or soon after, 1660 and which has belonged to the Mauritshuis, The Hague since 1822. It portrays the town of Delft, seen from the southwest, in the light of the early morning sun. There are two town gates on the other side of the water. The one on the left is the Schiedam gate with a clock in the roof gable indicating the time between seven o'clock and half past seven. The clock was used by ferryboats leaving the harbour to go to Rotterdam, Schiedam or Delfshaven. The men and women in the foreground on the left of the painting are waiting for the tow barge to leave its moorings. The other gate is the Rotterdam gate, where members of the seamen's guild used to meet. The building consisted of two parts. The gate itself, beautifully ornamented on the town side, can be seen on the right of the tower of the Nieuwe Kerk. Next to it is a watch path which ends in the outer gate with two small round turrets. The Rotterdam gate had kept much of its late mediaeval character in the seventeenth century. The drawbridge by the outer gate opens onto the east bank of the river Schie. The Schiedam gate also originally had a watch path with an outer gate. There was a triangular bastion by the outer gate, surrounded by water and linked to the Schiedam gate by a drawbridge. This bastion was constructed in 1573, when the fortifications were modernised. In 1614 it was dug up again, creating a triangular harbour called the Kolk. The outer gate and watch path of the Schiedam gate were also demolished, so that the building lost its original status of town gate. The spire of the Oude Kerk can be seen on the left in *View of Delft* with the slender tower of De Papegaey (the parrot) brewery to the right of it. The high, elongated roof to the left of the painting is also part of this huge brewery. The town wall runs alongside the water of the Kolk,

Coenraad Decker, The Armamentarium, *c. 1680*
Delft record office

with some of the façades of houses in the Kethelstraat rising
up behind it. The red roof of the Armamentarium is visible
above the bridge of the Rotterdam gate. Built in 1602, the
Armamentarium was the armoury of the States of Holland
and West Friesland. To the right of the Armamentarium is the
tower of the Nieuwe Kerk, where members of the House of
Orange-Nassau lie buried. The fact that the tower is bathed in
bright sunlight may be a subtle expression of support for the
stadholder and his family. Vermeer's painting radiates deep
tranquillity. Just as in *The little street*, the human figures are
unobtrusive in their surroundings. X-ray photographs and restoration work in 1994 revealed that Vermeer originally added
a seventh figure to the painting, which he later painted over. In
contrast with most other seventeenth century townscapes
there is hardly any sign of human activity. In this respect
Vermeer's painting is a misrepresentation of reality, as in the
seventeenth century the Kolk was a busy harbour. The Schie

View of Delft, *c. 1660-1661 (detail)*
The Hague, Mauritshuis

canal linked Delft with Rotterdam, Schiedam and Delfshaven: the latter had served as the real harbour of Delft since 1389 and was controlled by Delft town council. The Delft Chamber of the East India Company had its shipyards here, its East Indiamen were built here and its ships moored here on their return to the Republic from the East with their precious cargo. Barges carried the goods from Delfshaven to the Kolk.

Vermeer may have made use of devices such as the camera lucida or camera obscura when he painted View of Delft. These devices were already known in Antiquity, but were first used as an aid in the depiction of topographical scenes in the sixteenth century. With a camera lucida, a scene was projected onto a piece of paper or a plate of glass via a lens, as in photography, and the artist then copied the result. A camera obscura was a darkened room with a small hole in one wall, through which light reflected from an exterior scene can be projected to form an inverted image on the opposite wall. The camera lucida produces certain effects, such as a blurred perspective, intensified light and distorted reflections of light, particularly at the edges. But the role of the camera lucida in Vermeer's work may not be overestimated. He certainly did not trace the projected image, but he may have used both camera obscura and lucida to achieve special effects of light and colouring.

P.T.A. Swillens, who also turned his attention to the locality of *The little street*, was so impressed by the detailed depiction of the situation around the Kolk that he was sure the picture could only have been painted outside on the site. As the Hooikade was nowhere raised and the viewpoint of the painting is considerably above street level, Swillens was convinced that Vermeer must have worked from a building. A town plan of Delft from 1649 shows that the Hooikade was not yet built up in the mid seventeenth century, except where the Kolk enters the Schie, and that is the exact viewpoint of the painting. There was a little house on that very spot.

According to Swillens, Vermeer must have taken up his position on the first floor here and then painted the scene from nature. There is no sign of this house on the Figurative Map made between 1675 and 1678 but it shows that there were several houses on the Hooikade.

Vermeer could also have worked from one of these premises. Swillens' conception is not very plausible. There is not a single seventeenth-century artist who is known to have painted directly from nature. This was not done until the nineteenth century, when the French Impressionists were the first to set up their easels in the open air. Previously paintings were always completed in the artist's studio, sometimes based on sketches made earlier. Moreover, almost all seventeenth-century townscapes and landscapes were made from a higher viewpoint.

In those days, artists were most skilful in adapting the perspective. Comparison with other drawings and prints of the two gates shows that Vermeer adjusted the situation in the painting. The bridge over the Oude Delft between the two gates slopes upwards slightly in some of the drawings, while the bridge in Vermeer's painting is perfectly horizontal. The tower of the Nieuwe Kerk is slightly lower in relation to the other buildings than it is in reality. The houses to the left of the Schiedam gate have been raised in comparison with those on the right. Combined with the red and brown colouring, which dominates this part of the painting, a more or less continuous image emerges on the left-hand side, in which details such as the passage through the town wall next to the Schiedam gate can hardly be seen. The reason for these modifications could be that Vermeer did not want to disturb the horizontal scheme. The distance between both gates also seems to have increased for reasons of composition. X-ray photographs of the painting also reveal that Vermeer modified the reflection of the outer gate on the right. The two small turrets were completely reflected in the water originally, but Vermeer later altered the reflection so that the tops of the two spires remain out of sight. Vermeer's View of Delft is part of a long tradition of townscapes. Hendrick Vroom, Jan van Goyen, Daniel Vosmaer and Jan de Vos all painted their own versions of the Delft profile before him. They began by painting the north or west side of the town. According to the American art historian Alan Chong, Vermeer's decision to paint the town from the south may have been prompted by three events, which occurred shortly before the picture was painted.

The explosion in 1654 of the powder magazine of the States of Holland and West Friesland devastated most of the northeast of the town. When Vermeer painted his View of Delft six years later, the town had largely recovered but there were still some signs of the disaster.

After the explosion the town council issued a ban on the construction or equipping of powder magazines in or near the town. But small depots were left in two parts of the town, each with a modest supply for immediate use. One of these depots

was housed in the Armamentarium, visible in the painting with the sun shining on its roof. Fire broke out in this building in January 1660. Although the fire was soon under control, the people of Delft were not at all happy with the situation.

In the same year as this fire there was another event in the south of town, (the subject of Vermeer's painting) which made a deep impression on the people of Delft.

Charles II of England, who had been living in exile on the continent since the execution of his father Charles 1, heard when in Breda on 8th May 1660 that the English parliament had assented to his return to England. On his way to The Hague he would be passing through Delft and the town had prepared a great reception for him near the brand-new powder magazine of the Generality by the Schie. Charles II arrived at the site on the outskirts of town on the 25th May 1660. As he was early, there was no one there to meet him and he decided to continue on his way to Delft. The burghers of Delft, in great haste, eventually met him by the Rotterdam gate.

It would be going too far to link these three events directly with Vermeer's townscape. The destruction of the north-eastern part of the town had made Delft unattractive from the traditional viewpoint, while this important and festive occasion took place in the southwest just before the *View of Delft* was painted. Vermeer's masterpiece displays the splendour of Delft, as magnificent as ever in spite of the disaster.

There is little left of the splendour portrayed by Vermeer in or soon after 1660. Both of the gates and the town wall were pulled down in the eighteen thirties and the many stepped-gables in the painting have been replaced by modern fronts in the meantime. Only the towers of the Nieuwe Kerk and the Oude Kerk have survived. The present spire of the Nieuwe Kerk dates from 1875, as the original wooden spire caught fire when it was struck by lightning three years earlier.

The busy road, which now crosses the site of the fortifications, evokes a completely different atmosphere from the serenity which distinguishes the *View of Delft*. It would be better to avoid 'plein Delftzicht' if you are in search of the quietude in Vermeer's masterpiece.

6 The Death of the Artist

The 'Oude Kerk (the Old Church)

Vermeer was buried in the Oude Kerk, the oldest parish church in Delft. The church was first dedicated to St. Bartholomew, the patron saint of the founder of the church, Bartholomeus van der Made. Named after St. Hippolytus in 1396, a church founder and a martyr, the building was consecrated for Protestant worship from 1573 onwards.

Vermeer's mother-in-law, Maria Thins, bought a grave in the Oude Kerk in 1661. Although the church was used for Protestant worship, Catholics could also be buried there. It is written in Maria Thins' will that she did this to keep her funeral expenses down. Her original plan was to be buried in the St. Jan at Gouda. By purchasing her grave in Delft, she saved the fare to Gouda.

One of Vermeer's children was buried in the grave on 10th July 1667. This happened again in 1669 and again in 1673. He had already buried a child once before, in another grave. The names of the children are not given in the register of burials, so they must have died in early infancy. Fourteen years after Maria Thins bought the grave, her son-in-law Vermeer was also buried in it. The Oude Kerk register of burials records that he was buried on 16th December 1675. The coffin of the last of his children to die was placed on top of his coffin.

The artist's death may have been caused by the pressing financial problems which dogged him and his family. His widow wrote a petition to the Hof van Holland in 1677, for money to be released from his estate. In it she explains that as an art dealer, Vermeer was unable to sell the paintings in which he traded as a result of the war which had broken out with England and France in 1672, a year of crises for the Dutch. She writes "he was so laden with care for his many children and which he took so much to heart that it drove him to a frenzy, and from being alive and well the one day, within one and a half days he was dead.' Vermeer had probably become so agitated by his hopeless situation that he suffered a fatal heart attack. His brother-in-law Willem Bolnes also died a few months later and was buried in the same grave.

The situation remained very bleak for Vermeer's wife and children after his death. The loans and gifts from her mother Maria Thins brought no lasting solution. Maria died in December 1680 and she was buried in the family grave on 21st December. The grave was then full. Catharina and her children went to live in Breda after her mother died. In 1687 she visited her eldest daughter Maria, who married a silk merchant in 1674 and lived in the house called 'De Blauwe Hant' (the blue hand) on the Verwersdijk. There she fell ill and died soon afterwards. A note in the margin of the register of burials tells us that her coffin was carried by twelve bearers, an unusually high number. It is not (yet) known where Vermeer's widow was buried.

The location of Vermeer's grave was long unknown. The Delft historian A. van Peer succeeded in locating it in 1968. Churchwardens' accounts show that the grave purchased by Maria Thins in 1661 lay in the northern part of the church, the eighth grave in the second square. A square denotes a row of graves running from the wall to the nave. As this part of the church contained twenty-five rows of sixteen graves each, it was possible to single out the exact location of the grave. In 1975 a memorial tablet commemorating the third centenary of Vermeer's death was unveiled by Burgomaster Oele. He vacuumed a layer of sawdust from the tablet, symbolising the dust of ages. The remains of Vermeer and his family no longer lie under the stone. Most of the graves in the Oude Kerk have been cleared in the course of time, due to the danger of subsidence.

The grave of the renowned physicist Antoni van Leeuwenhoek (1632-1723) can also be found in the Oude Kerk. He was born a few days after Vermeer and their names happen to be on the same page of the register of births of the Nieuwe Kerk. He was appointed curator of Vermeer's estate after his death. Van Leeuwenhoek was buried in the Oude Kerk in 1723. The monument erected to him by his daughter in 1739 is a plain column with a medallion of the deceased on it.

The Chamber of Charity

The Chamber of Charity was the municipal charitable institution which supported those inhabitants of Delft in financial difficulties, either with money or in kind. This institution had been housed in a part of the Prinsenhof since 1614. The statue above the entrance in the Schoolstraat, which was probably made by Hendrick de Keyser, is a reminder of this.

It was the custom in the seventeenth century when someone died that the Chamber of Charity sent a chest to his house in which to collect the 'best garment' or a donation of equal value for the poor of the town. The register of the Chamber reveals that no chest was sent to Vermeer's house when he died because, it reads 'there is nothing to collect'. These few words express the deplorable financial situation of Vermeer's family at the time of his death.

The Chamber of Charity was directed by the masters of charity, an office which Vermeer's greatest collector, P.C. van Ruijven, also held between 1668 and 1672.

Van Ruijven was a wealthy Delft man of leisure who had grown rich from inheritances and wise investments. He was a passionate art lover who owned about twenty paintings by Vermeer. Vermeer was on good terms with Van Ruijven, who lent the artist two hundred guilders in 1657, perhaps as an advance on one or two paintings. Maria de Knuijt, the wife of Pieter van Ruijven, made a will in 1665 in which a further five hundred guilders was bequeathed to Vermeer.

When Vermeer died, his widow Catharina Bolnes was left with many debts. As a result of the war with France and England in

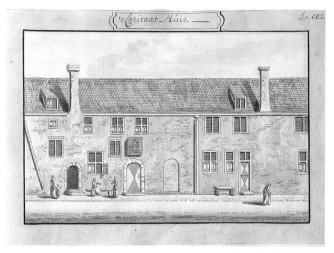

Abraham Rademaker, The Chamber of Charity, *c, 1700*
Delft record office

1672, Vermeer lost much of his income as he could not sell paintings. He was forced to borrow money which he had not yet repaid when he died. He owed the baker Hendrick van Buyten six hundred and seventeen guilders and six stuivers, which amounted to a three-year supply of bread. His widow paid this sum by selling two paintings by Vermeer: the *Lady writing a letter with her maid* and probably also *The guitar player*. Twenty-six paintings were transferred to the draper Jannetje Stevens, not Vermeer's own works but others which he, as an art dealer, had in his possession. Soon afterwards Jannetje sold these works to Jan Coelenbier, an art dealer from Haarlem, for five hundred guilders.

These paintings probably constituted the bulk of Vermeer's stock. To ensure that the remaining debts were also paid, a notary's clerk made an inventory of Catharina's belongings three months after the Vermeer's death . Just before this she visited a notary at The Hague to declare that she had given the painting *The allegory of painting* to her mother, along with the income from two rural estates. The transfer was a partial repayment of the money which she owed her mother. But this transaction was initially intended to keep some of her income and this particular painting by her husband, which she seems to have valued highly, from falling into the hands of the creditors.

At the end of April 1676 Catharina petitioned the Hof van Holland for postponement of payment, which was granted. Catharina was then declared bankrupt and she relinquished Vermeer's estate to the creditors. The Aldermen of Delft had to appoint someone to administer Catharina's affairs. The chosen curator was the well-known physicist Antoni van Leeuwenhoek who had been Chamberlain of Delft Aldermen since 1660, a combination of warden and bailiff.

In his spare time Van Leeuwenhoek made improvements to the microscope, through which he discovered the existence of red blood corpuscles, bacteria and spermatozoa. His famous contemporary, the Delft medical practitioner Reinier de Graaf (1641-1673), introduced Van Leeuwenhoek to the Royal Society in London. Van Leeuwenhoek kept this society informed of his microscopic discoveries in more than two hundred letters, with the result that he was made a Fellow of the Royal Society in 1680. Van Leeuwenhoek's interest in lenses and Vermeer's use of the camera obscura and lucida are sometimes interpreted as a sign that the two men knew each other. If that were true then the man in the paintings *The astronomer* and *The geographer* could be Van Leeuwenhoek, as he also studied mathematics, navigation and astronomy. But the way in which Van Leeuwenhoek administered the estate and his conflicts with Vermeer's widow and mother-in-law, suggest that he was more inclined to side with the creditors than with Vermeer's family. Van Leeuwenhoek was planning to organise an auction sale on 15th March 1677 in St. Luke's guildhall, to sell the twenty-six paintings in Vermeer's estate. He had reclaimed them from the draper Jannetje Stevens through a lawsuit. The picture *The allegory of painting* was also to be put up for auction, to the great displeasure of Maria Thins, who lodged a protest against this. It is not known whether the auction was actually held.

Van Leeuwenhoek makes his last appearance as curator in 1682. The guardian of Vermeer's children gave him permission to sell two bonds from the estate, possibly to pay the last outstanding debts to creditors.

Vermeer's work was also highly esteemed 9 years, after his death. One of the largest collections of his work belonged to the Delft printer Jacob Abrahamsz. Dissius, owner of the Gulden ABC printing office on the Markt. Dissius was married to Magdalena van Ruijven, the daughter and only heiress to Pieter Claesz. van Ruijven, the wealthy burgher of Delft who had bought many paintings directly from Vermeer during his lifetime. On Magdalena's death in 1682, the collection became the property of her husband. An inventory was made of all the pictures in his possession, which included as many as twenty paintings by Vermeer without mentioning their titles.
Jacob Dissius died in October 1695 and his collection of paintings was sold at auction in Amsterdam six months later. There were twenty-one Vermeers in the collection then, one more than was noted in the inventory made after the death of Magdalena. The paintings are described and mentioned by name in the auction catalogue. Famous paintings such as *The little street*, *The lace maker* and the View of Delft belonged to Jacob Dissius and graced his home at number 32 the Markt.

32, Markt. The house 'Het Gulden ABC' *of Jacob Dissius*

Vermeer's tombstone
At the memorial service for the third centenary of his
death the stone was placed on his grave in the Oude Kerk

The statue of The Milkmaid

The statue of *The milkmaid*, made by the artist Wim T. Schippers in Vermeer's honour was unveiled on 31st May 1976. The unveiling should really have taken place at the end of December 1975 to commemorate the third centenary of the artist's death, but it had to be postponed for five months due to all kinds of setbacks. The statue initially stood at the corner of the Phoenixstraat and the Schoolstraat, but it was later moved to the Binnenwatersloot. The statue is a stylised symbol of one of Vermeer's best-known paintings, *The milkmaid*, which was bought by the Rijksmuseum in Amsterdam in 1908. The work probably belonged to Pieter van Ruijven, later passing to the collection of paintings owned by his son-in-law Jacob Dissius. In the 1696 auction catalogue of Dissius' collection it is called A Maid pouring Milk and it is described as being 'uytnemende goet' or excellent. The painting has always been much admired and widely known, according to a catalogue of 1719 in which it is called *The famous milkmaid by Vermeer of Delft*. The painting is regarded as a simplified version of the Delft kitchen genre which was very popular in the Netherlands during the sixteenth century, but only continued in the seventeenth century at Delft.

The milkmaid is the only painting by Vermeer which portrays an ordinary person going about her everyday duties. His other paintings usually depict wealthy ladies and gentlemen at their leisure.

Vermeer used the technique called pointillism in this work, whereby images are built up by means of small dots. This style strives to portray as closely as possible what the eye sees. The human eye interprets surfaces which catch the sunlight in

The milkmaid,
c. 1658-1660
Amsterdam,
Rijksmuseum

The statue of **the milkmaid**. *From the artist Wim T. Schippers,*
made to commemorate the third centenary of Vermeer's death

shady surroundings, as patches and shining dots. This technique was applied especially in depicting the loaf of bread on the table. On the basis of this, the painting is dated about 1658-1660.

The little street and the *View of Delft* were also painted during this period. Vermeer used pointillism in the latter painting to highlight parts with the sun shining on them. The little statue of *The milkmaid* is a poor substitute for a Vermeer of its own, which Delft lacks. Most of Vermeer's paintings are in public collections, currently abroad. Only the Rijksmuseum in Amsterdam and the Mauritshuis in The Hague have some of his works. It is a bitter thing for Delft to accept that not only have most of the buildings linked with Vermeer disappeared, but the town does not even own a single painting by its most illustrious son.

Lady with a glass of wine , *ca. 1660-1661*
Berlijn, Staatliche Museum
zu Berlin, Gemäldegalerie.

Woman reading a letter at an
open window, *c. vers 1657*
Dresden, Staatliche
Kunstsammlungen, Gemäldegalerie
Alte Meister

Soldier and a
laughing girl,
c. 1658-1660
New York, The
Frick Collection

The girl with the wineglass,
c. 1659-1660
Braunschweig, Herzog Anton
Ulrich Museum

Girl with a red hat, *c. 1665*
Washington, The National Gallery of Art,
Andrew Mellon collection

The music-lesson
interrupted
c. 1660-1661
New York, The Frick
collection

Lady in yellow writing a letter, *c.1665*
Washington, the National Gallery of Art

The concert, *c. 1665-1666*
Boston, Isabella Stewart Gardner Museum
(Bridgeman Art Library)

Lady writing a letter and a maid, *c. 1670*
Dublin, The National Gallery of Ireland

Girl with flute, *ca. 1665-1670*
The National Gallery of Art, Wahington,
Wiedener collectie

Portrait of a young woman,
c. 1666-1667
New York, the Metropolitan
Museum of Art

Bibliography

Alpatow, M.W., 'Die Straße in Delft von Jan Vermeer, *Studien zur Geschichte der Westeuropäischen Kunst* (Cologne 1974) 142-144 and 193-203.

Alpers, S., *The Art of Describing: Dutch Art in the Seventeenth Century* (Chicago 1983).

Arasse, D., *Vermeer, faith in painting* (Princeton 1994).

Berckel, H.E. van, 'Priesters te Delft en Delfshaven, 1641-1696', in: *Haarlemsche bijdragen, bouwstoffen voor de Geschiedenis van het Bisdom Haarlem* 25 (1900) 230-263.

Beresteyn, E.A. van, *Grafmonumenten en grafzerken in de Oude Kerk te Delft* (Assen 1938).

Blankert, A., J. M. Montias and G. Aillaud, *Vermeer* (New York 1988).

Blankert, A., 'Vermeers Gezicht op Delft', *Kunstschrift* 38 (1994) 48-49.

Bleyswijck, D. van, *Beschryvinge der Stadt Delft* 2 vols. (Delft 1667-1680).

Bouricius, L.G.N., 'Nog eens 'Het straatje van Vermeer', *Maandblad van het personeel der verbonden petroleummaatschappijen* 5 (1922) 209-210.

Breunesse, J., 'De schilderkunst van ca. 1650 tot ca. 1670' in: *De Stad Delft, cultuur en maatschappij van 1572 tot 1667*. Exhibition catalogue Stedelijk Museum Het Prinsenhof (Delft 1981) 181-190.

Brink Goldsmith, J. ten et al., Leonaert Bramer 1596-1674. *Ingenious painter and draughtsman in Rome and Delft* (Zwolle/Delft 1994).

Broos, B., 'Gezicht op Delft', *Meesterwerken in het Mauritshuis* (The Hague 1987).

Broos, B. et al., *Johannes Vermeer*. Exhibition catalogue National Gallery and Mauritshuis (Washington/The Hague 1995).

Chong, A., Johannes Vermeer, *Gezicht op Delft* (Bloemendaal 1992).

Costaras, N. and J. Wadum, 'Vermeers gerestaureerd. Verseeckert sijn van altijt te duyren', *Natuur & Techniek* 63 (1995) 670-681

Goudappel, C.D., *Delftse Historische Sprokkelingen. Grepen uit de geschiedenis van Delft en omstreken* (Delft 1977).

Gout, M. and M.A. Verschuyl, *Stadhuis Delft* (Delft 1988).

Haaften, C.J. van, Nieuwe Langendijk: *Bouwhistorisch en archeologisch onderzoek van de panden 22 t/m 28* 3 vols. (Delft 1987).

Heijbroek, J.F. and W.Th. Kloek, 'Het straatje' van Vermeer, een geschenk van H.W.A. Deterding', *Bulletin van het Rijksmuseum* 40 (1992) 225-231.

Hengel, F. ten, 'Waag, Vleeshal en Lucasgilde' in: *De Stad Delft, cultuur en maatschappij van 1572 tot 1667*. Exhibition catalogue Stedelijk Museum Het Prinsenhof (Delft 1981) 56-58.

Hoeck, F. van, -De Jezuieten-Statie te Delft, 1592-1709-1771' in: *Haarlemsche bijdragen, Bouwstoffen voor de Geschiedenis van het Bisdom Haarlem* 60 (1948) 407-444.

Kaldenbach, C.J., 'Gezicht op Delft in de 17e en 18e eeuw' in: *De Stad Delft, cultuur en maatschappij van 1667 tot 1813*. Exhibition catalogue Stedelijk Museum Het Prinsenhof (Delft 1982-1983) 132-135.

Kersten, M., 'Jan van Goyens 'Gezicht op Delft vanuit het noorden, 1654', *Delfia Batavorum jaarboek* (1992) 61-76.

Krogt, P. van der and R. van der Krogt, *Gevelstenen in Delft* (Alphen aan den Rijn 1985).

Kunz, G.G., 'Alsof het hemelgewelf barstte en de aardbodem openscheurde. - .'in: H.L. Houtzager et al. ed., *Kruit en krijg: Delft als bakermat van het Prins Maurits Laboratorium TNO*. Publication of the Genootschap Delfia Batavorum no. 15 (Amsterdam 1988) 43-52.

Knevel, P., Burgers in het geweer. De schutterijen in Holland, 1550-1700 (Hilversum 1994). *Hollandse Studiën* 32.

Lindenburg, M.A., 'Het 'Straatje' van Vermeer', *Delfia Batavorum jaarboek* (1992) 77-88.

Lutz, E., Een kerk van honderd jaar, kroniek van een veelbewogen eeuw. *Gedenkschrift bij de gelegenheid van het 100 jarig bestaan van de Burgwalkerk te Delft* (Delft 1982).

Maarseveen, M.P. van, *In het voetspoor van Vermeer, een wandeling door Delft* (Delft 1995). Publication of VVV Delft.

Maarseveen, M.P. van, *Ach Lieve Tijd, 750 jaar Delft, Delftenaren en de Oranjes* 10 (Zwolle/Delft 1996).

Martin, W., 'Het straatje van Vermeer en de Six-stichting', *Oudheidkundig jaarboek* 1 (1921) 107-108.

Montias, J.M., *Artists and artisans in Delft, a socio-economic study of the seventeenth century* (Princeton 1982).

Montias, J.M., *Vermeer and his milieu: a web of social history* (Princeton 1989)

Nusselder, E.J., 'Het Oude Mannen- en het Oude Vrouwenhuis' in: *De Stad Delft, cultuur en maatschappij tot 1572*. Stedelijk Museum Het Prinsenhof Exhibition catalogue (Delft 1979-1980) 72-74.

Oosterloo, J.H. *De meesters van Delft* (Amsterdam 1948).

Palm, L.C., 'Antoni van Leeuwenhoek (1632-1723)' in: *De Stad Delft, cultuur en maatschappij van 1667 tot 1813*. Stedelijk Museum Het Prinsenhof Exhibition catalogue (Delft 1982-1983) 96-102.

Peer, A.J.J.M. van, 'Het Straatje van Vermeer', *Gids voor Delft en omstreken* (Delft 1952) 21-25.

Schneider, N., *Jan Vermeer* 1632-1675 (Cologne 1994).

Sluijter, E.J., 'De schilderkunst van ca. 1570 tot ca. 1650' in: *De Stad Delft, cultuur en maatschappij van 1572 tot 1667*. Exhibition catalogue Stedelijk Museum Het Prinsenhof Exhibition catalogue (Delft 1981) 172-181.

Swillens, P.T.A., *Johannes Vermeer, painter of Delft 1632-1675* (Utrecht 1950).

Temminck Groll, C.L., 'Delft als stad van zestiende-eeuwse woonhuizen-' in: *Delftse Studiën* (Assen 1967) 62-114.

Veen, J., 'Boekbespreking', *Oud Holland* 106 (1992) 99-101.

Waals, J. van der, 'In het straatje van Montias, Vermeer in historische context, *Theoretische geschiedenis* 19 (1992) 176-185.

Wadum, J. et al., *Vermeer in het Licht. Conservering, Restauratie en Onderzoek* (Wormer 1994).

Weve, W.F., 'Woonhuizen' in: *De Stad Delft, cultuur en maatschappij tot 1572*. Stedelijk Museum Het Prinsenhof Exhibition catalogue (Delft 1979-1980) 74-80.

Weve, W.F., 'Stadspoorten-' in: *De Stad Delft, cultuur en maatschappij tot 1572.* Stedelijk Museum Het Prinsenhof Exhibition catalogue (Delft 1979-1980) 80-84.

Weve, W.F., 'Delftse woonhuizen' in: *De Stad Delft, cultuur en maatschappij van 1572 tot 1667.* Stedelijk Museum Het Prinsenhof Exhibition catalogue (Delft 1981) 60-62.

Weve, W.F., *Voorlopig rapport betreffende de panden Nieuwe Langendijk 22 t/m 26 als onderwerp van het schilderij 'het straatje' van Johannes Vermeer* (Delft 1982).

Wheelock, A.K., *Jan Vermeer* (New York 1981).

Wheelock, A.K. and C.J. Kaldenbach, 'Vermeer's View of Delft and his vision of reality', *Artibus et historiae* 6 (1982) 9-35.

Wheelock, A.K., 'History, Politics and the Portrait of a City: Vermeer's View of Delft' in: S. Zimmerman and R.F.E. Weissman ed., *Urban Life in the Renaissance* (Newark 1989) 165-184.

Wheelock, A.K., *Vermeer and the Art of Painting* (New Haven/London 1995).

Wijbenga, D., *De Oude Kerk van Delft, 750 jaar in woord en beeld* (Delft 1990).

Wright, C., *Vermeer* (London 1976).

In de miniaturenreeks zijn verschenen